AF593894

salads

Quadrille
PUBLISHING

This edition first published in 2009 by **Quadrille Publishing Limited**
Alhambra House, 27-31 Charing Cross Road, London WC2H 0LS

Editor Anne McDowall
Production Marina Asenjo

Most of the material in this book was previously published as Super Salads and also in **delicious.** magazine or **Sainsbury's Magazine**; it was provided courtesy of the Seven Publishing Group.

Cataloguing in Publication Data:
a catalogue record for this book is available from the British Library.

ISBN 978 184400 786 8
Printed in China

Cookery notes
All spoon measures are level unless otherwise stated: 1 teaspoon = 5 ml spoon; 1 tablespoon = 15 ml spoon. Use fresh herbs unless dried herbs are suggested. Use sea salt and freshly ground black pepper unless otherwise stated. Free-range eggs are recommended and large eggs should be used except where a different size is specified. Recipes which feature raw or lightly cooked eggs should be avoided by anyone who is pregnant or in a vulnerable health group.

Contents

6 introduction

8 **salads** starters & light salads

30 **salads** beef, pork & lamb

56 **salads** fish & shellfish

82 **salads** chicken, duck & game

108 **salads** veggie

128 **salads** sides

156 **salads** fruit

170 **salads** dressings & mayonnaise

190 index

192 acknowledgements

Introduction

The salad is one of the most flexible and adaptable dishes, offering the basis for infinite combinations of flavours and ingredients. From the light summer dishes we are familiar with to recipes for warm and hearty meals, the salads in this book cover the whole range – as well as a selection of fruit salads.

Salads proves there is more to this versatile dish than crisp lettuce and sliced tomato. The recipes here are inventive and diverse, making creative use of unexpected ingredients, such as duck, pheasant and roast lamb.

You'll find Spanish, Italian, Chinese, Thai and British influences vying for your attention, and the recipes are organised into chapters by their main ingredient for easy selection. There is also a final chapter on the techniques of making dressings and mayonnaises, with suggestions on what best to pair them with.

From the classic Greek salad, through tempting side-dishes, including a warm barley salad with butternut squash, to twists on traditional favourites and a large selection of substantial main courses, there is something here for every occasion all year round.

salads
starters & light salads

Parma ham, fig & mozzarella salad

Serves 2–3
50g rocket leaves
6 ripe figs
2 x 175g buffalo mozzarella balls
6 slices Parma ham
2 tbsp honey
2 tbsp lemon juice
freshly ground black pepper
2–3 pitta breads

1. Spread the rocket leaves onto a platter. Cut the figs in half and arrange on the leaves.
2. Tear the buffalo mozzarella and add to the platter. Tear the Parma ham slices into strips and arrange on the platter.
3. Mix the honey with the lemon juice and drizzle over the top. Season with black pepper.
4. Pop a few pitta breads in the toaster and serve warm with the salad.

Warm chicken & herb salad

Serves 2

3 chicken breasts, skins removed
2 tbsp olive oil
110g fine green beans, trimmed and halved
20g fresh parsley, leaves only
20g fresh mint, leaves only
2 tbsp Dijon mustard
2 tbsp capers, drained
1 tbsp balsamic vinegar
100g mixed salad leaves
salt and freshly ground black pepper

1. Heat a griddle pan and boil the kettle. Cut the chicken into thickish strips and toss with 1 tsp of the oil and some seasoning.
2. Cook the chicken for 4 minutes on each side. Meanwhile, cook the beans in boiling water until tender, then drain.
3. Place the parsley, mint, mustard, capers, balsamic vinegar and the rest of the olive oil in a food processor and whiz together.
4. Toss the hot chicken strips and beans with the salad leaves and the dressing. Serve immediately.

This also works well using chunks of griddled salmon. For extra sustenance, serve with some warm, crusty bread.

Vietnamese salad

Illustrated on the following pages

Serves 4
2 large chicken breasts, skins removed
2 tbsp vegetable oil
4 tbsp peanuts, chopped
2 shallots, thinly sliced
1 head Chinese leaf
225g carrots, grated
6 spring onions, shredded
4 tbsp chopped fresh mint
25g bunch fresh coriander

For the dressing
2 red chillies, deseeded and chopped
3 garlic cloves, crushed
2 tbsp brown sugar
1 tbsp rice vinegar
juice of 1 large or 2 small limes
1 tbsp fish sauce
3 tbsp vegetable oil

1. Put the dressing ingredients in a bowl and whisk well. Set aside.
2. Brush the chicken breasts with 1 tbsp vegetable oil and cook on a hot griddle pan over a medium heat for about 5 minutes on each side, or until cooked through. Set aside to rest for 5 minutes, then cut into large strips.
3. For the salad, heat 1 tbsp vegetable oil in a small pan and fry the peanuts for 1–2 minutes, until golden. Remove with a slotted spoon and drain on kitchen paper. Set aside.
4. Add the shallots to the oil and fry for 3–4 minutes, until golden and crisp. Drain on kitchen paper and set aside.
5. Tear the Chinese leaf into pieces and put in a large bowl. Add the carrot, spring onions and mint. Toss well and spoon onto a large platter. Drizzle with the dressing and toss together. Scatter with the coriander, peanuts and shallots. Serve with the chicken strips.

All-day-breakfast salad

Serves 2

2 large, very fresh eggs
8 rashers smoked streaky bacon
1 baguettine or small French stick
12 cherry tomatoes, halved
150g mixed salad leaves, including frisée
2 tbsp French dressing (see the recipe on page 172)

1. Pour 2.5cm of boiling water into a small frying pan and bring back to a very gentle simmer.
2. Gently break in the eggs, leave for 1 minute and then take off the heat. Leave for 10 minutes while you prepare the rest of the salad.
3. Fry the bacon in a large non-stick frying pan until brown and crisp. Leaving the fat in the pan, transfer the bacon onto some kitchen paper.
4. Slice the baguettine into six thin slices (you will have some left over) and then cut each slice in half. Fry in the bacon fat until it is crisp on both sides.
5. Put the tomatoes into a large bowl with the salad leaves and dressing. Chop the bacon and add to the bowl along with the warm croutons.
6. Toss together, divide between two plates and top with the poached eggs. Serve with the extra bread on the side.

Tomato, fresh mint & lemon salad

Serves 6

700g tomatoes, using a mixture of Pomodorino, Sungold, midi, plum and Flavia tomatoes
110g sun-blushed tomatoes
large handful fresh mint, roughly shredded
zest of 1 lemon, juice of half
4 tbsp extra-virgin olive oil
½ tsp caster sugar
salt and freshly ground black pepper

1. Cut all the tomatoes into bite-sized pieces. Combine them in a bowl, mix in the lemon zest and set aside for 1 hour.
2. Meanwhile, make a dressing by whisking together the lemon juice, olive oil, seasoning and the sugar.
3. To serve, pour the dressing over the tomatoes, add the mint and mix well to combine.

Zesty herb & chilli crab salad with crostini

Serves 6

1 small baguette, thinly sliced diagonally into 18 pieces
75ml extra-virgin olive oil, plus extra for brushing
juice of ½ small lemon, plus wedges to serve
handful fresh chives, finely chopped
few sprigs fresh dill, finely chopped
3 tbsp finely chopped fresh parsley leaves
2 red chillies, deseeded, 1 finely chopped, 1 finely sliced
300g fresh white crabmeat, any shell discarded
150g mixed baby salad leaves
salt and freshly ground black pepper

Note: You will also need a 9cm ring mould or pastry cutter.

1. Preheat the grill to medium. For the crostini, place half the baguette slices on a large baking tray, season and brush all over with olive oil. Grill for about 1 minute each side, until golden. Set aside on a wire rack to cool and repeat with the remaining baguette.
2. In a bowl, mix together 75ml oil, the lemon juice, fresh herbs and chopped red chilli. Season to taste and set aside to infuse for 5 minutes.
3. Put the crabmeat into a large bowl and gradually mix in just over half of the herb mixture to bind. Season to taste.
4. Place the ring mould or pastry cutter on a plate. Press in some of the crab mix, then remove the ring. Repeat to make six starters.
5. To serve, top each with a small pile of salad leaves. Garnish with the sliced chilli, drizzle around the remaining herb oil and serve with the crostini and lemon wedges to squeeze over.

Classic Caesar salad

Serves 6
3 slices rye bread
1 garlic clove, crushed
3 tbsp olive oil
4 Little Gem lettuces, leaves separated
50g fresh Parmesan
6 tbsp Caesar salad dressing (see the recipe on page 182)
sea salt

1. First make the croutons for the salad. Preheat the oven to 200°C (fan 180°C), gas 6. Cut the crusts off the bread, then cut the bread into small pieces. Put into a roasting tin, sprinkle with the garlic, olive oil and a little sea salt, and mix together. Cook for 10 minutes. Leave to cool until needed.
2. Rinse the lettuce in a colander under cold running water. Shake dry.
3. Put a handful of the lettuce leaves in a bowl (tearing any large leaves) and sprinkle with the croutons.
4. Drag a vegetable peeler over the Parmesan and let a few shavings fall into the salad. Drizzle over some Caesar salad dressing.

To make this into a more substantial dish try adding small pieces of grilled bacon or strips of griddled chicken.

Paula

Tomato, peach & cumin salad

Serves 2
2 ripe peaches
4 large ripe tomatoes
½ tsp cumin seeds
2 garlic cloves, finely sliced
juice of ½ lemon
2 tbsp extra-virgin olive oil, plus extra to drizzle
8 fresh mint leaves, to garnish
salt and freshly ground black pepper
200g Feta or goats' cheese, to serve

1. Skin the peaches and tomatoes in the same way. Score the stalk ends with an 'X'. Plunge into boiling water for 20 seconds, then transfer to cold water. As soon as they are cool enough to handle, peel away the skins. Stone the peaches, deseed the tomatoes and cut both into wedges. Transfer to a bowl.
2. Heat a frying pan or wok. Dry-fry the cumin seeds for about 30 seconds, until they start to smell roasted – you cannot mistake the aroma. Roughly crush them in a pestle and mortar, then add to the peaches and tomatoes with the garlic.
3. Whisk the lemon juice and olive oil with some salt and pepper into a salad dressing. Toss through the salad. Allow the salad to sit for up to an hour.
4. To serve, garnish with mint leaves and some crumbled Feta or goats' cheese that has been drizzled with olive oil.

Once you've tried this, you'll be hooked. It also makes a great accompaniment to grilled fish, shellfish and meat dishes.

Crab, avocado & crispy bacon salad

Serves 2

135g mixed salad of watercress, rocket and spinach
1 ripe avocado, stoned, peeled and sliced
30g toasted pine nuts
40g cooked crispy bacon
100g fresh white crabmeat
3 tbsp olive oil
1 tbsp lemon juice
salt and freshly ground black pepper

1. Divide the salad between two large serving plates. Dot over the avocado, pine nuts and broken up pieces of crispy bacon. Top with the crabmeat.
2. In a small bowl, whisk together the olive oil and lemon juice. Season to taste and drizzle over the salad to serve.

If you can't source fresh crabmeat then use a 170g can of crabmeat, drained, instead.

Sticky spare ribs & crunchy slaw

Serves 6

1.5kg pork spare ribs
6 tbsp dark soy sauce
3 tbsp kecap manis
4 tbsp honey
60g fresh ginger, sliced into thick rounds
4 spring onions
3 tbsp Chinese rice wine or sherry vinegar

For the crunchy slaw

6 spring onions, thinly sliced
1 large carrot, cut into short, thin strips
1 small cucumber, cut into short, thin strips
2 tbsp mayonnaise (see the recipe on page 186)
3 tbsp olive oil
juice of 1 lime, plus extra lime wedges, to serve
salt and freshly ground black pepper

1. Put the spare ribs in a large non-stick roasting tin. Mix the soy sauce, kecap manis and honey in a bowl and pour over the ribs. Add the ginger, whole spring onions and rice wine.
2. Put the tin on the hob, pour over 1 litre of water and bring to the boil. Cover with foil and simmer over a medium heat for 45 minutes, turning regularly to ensure the ribs cook evenly.
3. Put all the slaw ingredients in a serving bowl, season, and toss well.
4. Remove and discard the ginger and spring onions from the rib mixture. Increase the heat to high and cook, uncovered, for a further 30–40 minutes, until the sauce is thick and syrupy. Once cooked, the ribs should be evenly coated with a dark glaze and the meat should be very tender.
5. To serve, pile the ribs and pan juices on a platter, put the bowl of slaw alongside and serve with the lime wedges to squeeze over.

The crunchy slaw makes a lovely contrast to those finger-licking sticky ribs. Kecap manis is an Indonesian sweet soy sauce.

Squid, lemon & caper salad

Serves 4

600g squid, cleaned, gutted and cut into rings (ask your fishmonger to do this)
juice of 3 unwaxed lemons, with their leaves if possible, plus extra lemon wedges to serve
2 tbsp capers, soaked and rinsed if packed in salt
3 garlic cloves, finely sliced
5 whole black peppercorns
40g pitted Kalamata, halved, or whole small black olives
100ml extra-virgin olive oil
salt

1. Put a generous handful of salt into a large pan of water and bring to a rolling boil. Blanch the squid in the pan for no more than 30 seconds, then drain. Alternatively, sear it on a ridged griddle or cast-iron frying pan for about 30 seconds on either side.
2. Using a potato peeler or fruit knife, peel four or five strips of lemon zest and put them in a mixing bowl. If the lemons have leaves, destalk and shred two of them to add to the zest. (You could use bay leaves instead.)
3. Add the capers to the bowl with the lemon juice, garlic, peppercorns, olives and oil. Mix thoroughly, then stir in the squid while still warm. Cover and marinate in the fridge, ideally overnight.
4. Serve with lemon wedges. It shouldn't need salt but check to make sure.

This is actually best made a day ahead, so is good for entertaining. It is great served with thin slices of fennel or chicory, on toast or tossed with some warm new potatoes.

Warm salad of pear, scallop & chorizo

Serves 4

100g chorizo, skinned and thinly sliced
12 fresh scallops, shucked and washed but whole with orange roe left on
2 medium, firm pears, cored and thinly sliced
1 tbsp sherry vinegar
75g bunch of watercress, washed and destalked
1 tbsp olive oil
salt

1. Make sure you have everything prepared before you start cooking. Gently heat a non-stick frying pan. When hot, add the chorizo and dry-fry until just beginning to brown – it will release its own oil after 30 seconds or so. Remove with a slotted spoon and set aside on kitchen paper.
2. Add the scallops to the pan and sear in the chorizo oil for about 1 minute each side. Remove and set aside with the chorizo.
3. Finally, add the pear slices and fry quite briskly to caramelise a little. Once you have turned them, add the vinegar and swirl the pears around in it for a few seconds, then tip it all into a bowl.
4. Add the scallops, chorizo, watercress and oil. Season with salt (not pepper in case the chorizo has a kick of its own). Serve immediately.

Be demanding when you shop for this recipe. You want a good chorizo (the thinner, dryer kind is best); firm pears (the harder the better); and look for diver-caught scallops.

salads beef, pork & lamb

Tagliata (seared steak & rocket salad)

Serves 2

400g small baby new potatoes
2 x 150g beef steaks, such as rib-eye or sirloin, about 2cm thick
1 tsp Dijon mustard
1 tbsp balsamic vinegar
1 tbsp capers
3 tbsp extra-virgin olive oil
1 tbsp finely chopped fresh tarragon
50g rocket leaves
salt and freshly ground black pepper

1. Boil the potatoes until tender, then drain. Allow to cool slightly.
2. Meanwhile, sear the steaks in a hot, dry frying pan for about 2 minutes each side (this will leave them rare, so if you prefer your meat medium-rare, make it 3 minutes each side). Rest the steaks once they are cooked.
3. Make the salad. Cut the still-warm potatoes in half (or break them up with your hands) and toss with the mustard, vinegar, capers, 2 tbsp extra-virgin olive oil and the tarragon.
4. Slice the steak as thinly as you can and toss it into the salad with the rocket. Season with salt, pepper and the remaining oil.

This is an Anglicised version of an Italian dish of rare, sliced steak dressed with balsamic vinegar. Hunt down some good beef, properly aged balsamic vinegar and early Jersey Royal potatoes to make this really special.

Griddled beef salad with mushrooms

Serves 2

1 tbsp capers, drained
2 cloves garlic, peeled and roughly chopped
2 tsp Dijon mustard
20g fresh flat-leaf parsley
20g fresh basil
6 tbsp olive oil
250g chestnut mushrooms
2 x 225g sirloin steaks
150g mixed herb salad
salt and freshly ground black pepper
crusty bread, to serve

1. Put the capers, garlic, mustard, parsley, basil, 5 tbsp of olive oil and some black pepper in a small food processor; whiz to make a coarse purée. Thickly slice the mushrooms.
2. Heat a large griddle pan over a high heat. Brush both sides of the steaks with some of the remaining oil and season with pepper. Cook for 1–2 minutes on each side (they will be pink inside), pressing them on to the pan with a fish slice. Remove to a plate.
3. Add the mushrooms to the griddle along with the rest of the oil, if needed, and cook for 4 minutes, tossing now and then.
4. Slice the beef and sprinkle with sea salt. Toss the beef with its juices, the mushrooms, salad leaves and dressing together in a large bowl and serve with warm, crusty bread.

Hot Thai beef salad

Serves 2

1 garlic clove, chopped
1½ tsp brown sugar
1 tbsp lime juice
2 tbsp light soy sauce
½ cucumber
handful of beansprouts
1 red chilli, deseeded and finely sliced
large handful of mint leaves
1 Little Gem lettuce
2 x 150g sirloin or rump steaks
salt and freshly ground black pepper

1. First make the dressing. Chop the garlic clove and, in a bowl, whisk with the brown sugar, lime juice and soy sauce. Set aside.
2. Halve and deseed the cucumber, cut into sticks and put into a bowl. Deseed and finely slice the chilli and add to the bowl with the beansprouts, mint leaves and the torn-up leaves of the lettuce. Toss well and divide between two plates.
3. Heat a griddle, frying pan or grill. Season the steaks and cook them for 2–5 minutes on each side, depending on how well done you like them.
4. Place the steaks on a board and cut into slices. Divide between the plates and drizzle with the dressing.

Griddled steak with potatoes & peppers

Serves 2

315g new potatoes
2 x 200g sirloin steaks, trimmed
150g mixed pepper antipasto, drained and chopped, the oil marinade reserved
25g wild rocket leaves
1 tbsp small capers, rinsed and drained
salt and freshly ground black pepper

1. Bring a pan of salted water to the boil. Cook the potatoes for 15 minutes until tender.
2. Meanwhile, brush the steaks with 2 tbsp of the marinade from the peppers. Season with black pepper and leave to one side for 5 minutes.
3. Heat a griddle pan until very hot, then fry the steaks for 3 minutes on each side, remove to a board and leave to rest for 5 minutes.
4. Drain the potatoes and, when cool enough to handle, thickly slice them into a bowl. Add the rocket, capers, peppers and 2 tbsp of the pepper marinade. Season and toss together.
5. Season the steaks with a little salt, slice them in half and serve on top of the salad. Drizzle with any extra juices.

Warm new potato & smoked sausage salad

Illustrated on the following pages

Serves 4

600g anya or baby new potatoes
2 x 225g packs smoked pork sausage or frankfurter
1 small red onion, peeled, halved and thinly sliced into half moons
20g fresh dill, fronds chopped
4 large handfuls rocket leaves
salt

For the dressing

1½ tbsp Dijon mustard
3 tbsp red-wine vinegar
2 tsp caster sugar
2 tbsp small capers
6 tbsp extra-virgin olive oil
salt and freshly ground black pepper

1. Cook the new potatoes for 10–15 minutes in boiling salted water until easily pierced with a knife.
2. Meanwhile, bring another pan of water to the boil and add the smoked sausage. Cook for 15 minutes, then cut into 1cm slices.
3. Place the dressing ingredients and some salt and pepper in a lidded jar. Shake well, then set aside.
4. Drain the potatoes and let them cool slightly before slicing. Place them in a medium bowl with the onion, dill and sausage.
5. Pour the dressing over and gently mix. Divide between four plates with a handful of rocket and serve.

Smoked pork sausage is surprisingly versatile. It keeps well in the fridge and is ideal for soups, sandwiches and salads.

Warm mozzarella, bacon & nectarine

Serves 4
250g diced bacon
4 tbsp olive oil
150g mozzarella
2 nectarines
2 tbsp sherry vinegar
2 tsp mustard
200g rocket salad
8 fresh mint leaves
salt and freshly ground black pepper

1. Fry the bacon in 1 tbsp olive oil until crispy. Drain on kitchen paper.
2. Drain the mozzarella and tear into pieces. Halve the nectarines, stone them, and slice each half into four.
3. In a small pan, whisk together the sherry vinegar, 3 tbsp olive oil and the mustard. Warm through.
4. Put the rocket salad in a large bowl and add the bacon and nectarines. Tear the mint leaves over the top.
5. Toss with the warm dressing, some seasoning and the mozzarella. Serve immediately.

Warm potato salad with Parma ham

Serves 6

2 large red peppers
600g Jersey Royal new potatoes, scrubbed
4 tsp extra-virgin olive oil, plus extra for drizzling
1 tbsp chopped fresh flat-leaf parsley
12 thin slices Parma ham
50g baby salad leaves
½ tsp white-wine vinegar

1. Preheat the oven to 220°C (fan 200°C), gas 7. Roast the whole peppers for 20–25 minutes, until lightly charred. Seal in a plastic bag and cool. Remove and discard the stalks, seeds and skin. Cut into strips.
2. Cook the potatoes in plenty of boiling, salted water for 10–12 minutes or until tender. Drain. When cool enough to handle, thickly slice into a large bowl. Fold in the oil and parsley.
3. To serve, ruffle two slices of Parma ham onto each plate, then pile over some of the salad leaves. Stir the vinegar into the potatoes, season, and arrange on top of the salad along with the red pepper strips. Drizzle over a little more oil and serve at once.

To get ahead you can prepare the peppers the day before and chill overnight. Bring them back up to room temperature before using.

BLT salad

Illustrated on the following pages

Serves 4

½ ciabatta
olive oil, for drizzling
10–12 rashers dry-cure smoked streaky bacon
85g wild rocket leaves
120g baby spinach leaves
16 cherry tomatoes, halved
salt and freshly ground black pepper

For the dressing

4 tbsp good mayonnaise (see the recipe on page 188)
1 small clove garlic, peeled and crushed
2 tsp grainy mustard
1 tbsp sherry vinegar
4 tbsp olive oil

1. Cut the bread into cubes, toss them in a little olive oil with some seasoning, and tip into a frying pan. Toast over a low heat for 4–5 minutes. Leave to cool.
2. Mix the dressing ingredients together in a bowl with 1 tbsp of cold water. Grill the bacon under a hot grill on both sides until really crispy, then halve widthways.
3. Toss the leaves in a bowl with the dressing. Divide between four bowls, layering with the tomatoes, croûtons and bacon as you go, and serve.

Paprika-spiced pork

Serves 4

3 small lemons
500g pork fillet (tenderloin), trimmed of all fat and cut into 32 small pieces
4 garlic cloves, crushed
1 tsp dried oregano
1 tsp each ground cumin, coriander and turmeric
2 tsp paprika
4 tbsp Greek yogurt
16 fresh bay leaves
16 pickled whole red chillies (optional)
3 red onions, thickly sliced
3 beef tomatoes, thickly sliced
1 tbsp olive oil
balsamic vinegar, for drizzling
large handful fresh flat-leaf parsley, roughly torn

Note: You will also need 8 metal skewers.

1. Finely grate the zest from 1 lemon and squeeze the juice. Put both into a bowl with the pork, garlic, oregano, ground spices and yogurt. Mix well, cover and set aside to marinate for at least 20 minutes (or up to 2 hours, if you have time).
2. Preheat the grill to hot. Cut each of the remaining lemons into eight wedges. Thread four pieces of pork, two wedges of lemon, two bay leaves and two chillies, if using, alternately on each skewer. Arrange on a large foil-lined grill tray and grill for 15 minutes, turning, until the pork is cooked through and lightly charred.
3. Meanwhile, preheat the oven to 180°C (fan 160°C), gas 4 and heat a large griddle pan until smoking. Brush the onions and tomatoes with the oil and season well. Chargrill the onions on the griddle for 5 minutes, turn them over and cook for a further 2 minutes. Transfer to a baking dish and keep hot in the oven while you cook the tomatoes. Add the tomatoes to the griddle pan and chargrill for 2–3 minutes, without turning.
4. Pile the tomatoes onto serving plates with the onions and sprinkle with some balsamic vinegar and flat-leaf parsley. Arrange the spiced pork skewers on top to serve.

Apple & pork salad with cider dressing

Serves 2
2 thick slices of bread
5 tbsp olive oil
200g pork tenderloin fillet
1 Cox's apple
1 tbsp cider vinegar
130g of salad leaves
salt and freshly ground black pepper

1. Cut off and discard the crusts from the bread. Cut the bread into cubes. Heat 3 tbsp olive oil in a frying pan and cook the bread for 4–5 minutes, tossing regularly. Drain on kitchen paper and set aside.
2. Trim any fat from the pork fillet and cut into six thick slices. Flatten each piece slightly.
3. Wipe out the frying pan with kitchen paper. Heat 1 tbsp olive oil in the pan and fry the pork for 5–6 minutes, turning once. Remove from the pan and set aside.
4. Cut the apple into twelve wedges and fry in the same pan for 1–2 minutes, turning once, until dark golden. Remove and set aside. Add the cider vinegar and 1 tbsp olive oil and sizzle briefly. Season well.
5. Toss the salad leaves with the homemade croutons and apple wedges and divide between two plates. Top with the pork and drizzle with the dressing.

Warm Sunday roast salad

Serves 6

2–2.5kg leg of lamb
4 garlic cloves, cut into slivers
few sprigs fresh rosemary
450g baby new potatoes
175ml olive oil
200g French green beans
4 tbsp red-wine vinegar
generous pinch of sugar
3 tbsp freshly chopped mint
600g cherry tomatoes, halved
350g baby spinach leaves, rocket or watercress, or a mixture
salt and freshly ground black pepper

1. Preheat the oven to 220°C (fan 200°C), gas 7. With the tip of a small, sharp knife make slits all over the lamb. Insert a sliver of garlic and a sprig of rosemary into each slit.

2. Weigh the lamb and calculate the cooking time. Cook for 20 minutes, then reduce the oven temperature to 190°C (fan 170°C), gas 5 and roast for a further 20 minutes per 450g. This will give a slightly pink lamb. Add an extra 20 minutes if you like it medium.

3. Meanwhile, cook the potatoes in boiling, salted water for 10–15 minutes, until tender. Drain and spill into a roasting tin, drizzle with 2 tbsp of oil and season. Roast for 30 minutes before the lamb is done.

4. Cook the beans in boiling, salted water, drain and refresh under cold running water. Drain again and set aside.

5. Make the dressing: whisk together the remaining oil, vinegar, sugar, mint and plenty of seasoning.

6. Take the lamb and potatoes out of the oven. Leave the lamb to rest for about 15 minutes and let the potatoes cool (they both only need to be just warm when served).

7. Slice the lamb and put on to a plate. Put the tomatoes, salad leaves, green beans and warm potatoes into a large bowl and toss well. Drizzle with enough dressing to coat and toss again. Add the lamb to serve. Put the rest of the dressing into a jug for everyone to help themselves.

Lamb & aubergine with pomegranate

Serves 4

For the marinade/dressing

6 tbsp pomegranate molasses
juice of ½ lemon
2 cloves garlic, peeled and crushed
6 tbsp extra-virgin olive oil
1 tsp caster sugar
salt and freshly ground black pepper

For the salad

600g lamb leg steaks
2 aubergines, cut into 2cm slices
2 tsp ground cinnamon
200g fine green beans, trimmed
3 tbsp roughly chopped flat-leaf parsley
1 small red onion, peeled and chopped
salt and freshly ground black pepper

To serve

4 tbsp Greek yogurt
4 pitta breads or flatbreads

1. Combine the marinade/dressing ingredients with some salt and pepper in a screw-top jar. Shake well and set aside.
2. Put the lamb steaks and aubergine slices into a large non-metallic dish. Season and sprinkle with the cinnamon. Pour a third of the marinade over both and mix together until thoroughly combined. Cover and marinate in the fridge for 3–4 hours. Remove from the fridge 45 minutes before cooking.
3. Blanch the green beans in boiling salted water for 3–4 minutes or until tender, then drain in a colander and rinse in cold water.
4. Heat the griddle pan until hot. Griddle the lamb steaks for 2–3 minutes on each side (this will give you pink lamb). Remove and leave the meat to rest for 5 minutes on a board.
5. While the lamb rests, griddle the aubergine in batches for 2–3 minutes on each side or until softened (discard any marinade on the aubergine). Arrange the aubergine in a dish. Toast the pitta breads lightly under the grill.
6. Slice the lamb and arrange over the aubergine. Sprinkle with the parsley, red onion and green beans then pour the remaining dressing over before serving with a bowl of Greek yogurt and the toasted pitta breads.

salads fish & shellfish

Seared tuna with bean & olive salad

Serves 3

410g can cannellini beans, drained and rinsed
1 small red onion, finely sliced
2 celery sticks, finely sliced
French dressing, for drizzling (see the recipe on page 172)
50g rocket leaves
3 fresh tuna steaks
2 tbsps olive oil
24 black olives
salt and freshly ground black pepper

1. Put the cannellini beans into a bowl. Add the red onion and the celery. Drizzle with a little French dressing and season well.
2. Divide the rocket between three serving plates and spoon the bean mix over the leaves.
3. Heat a griddle. Brush the tuna steaks with olive oil and fry on the griddle for 2–3 minutes each side.
4. Serve a tuna steak with each salad and scatter with the black olives.

You could replace the fresh tuna with a large can of tuna in oil, drained.

Tuna salad with beans, capers & new potatoes

Serves 2
2 tuna steaks
2 tbsp olive oil
2 tsp soy sauce
juice of ½ lemon
1 tbsp capers, rinsed and drained
handful fresh chives, chopped
350g small new potatoes
100g fine green beans
salt and freshly ground black pepper

1. Boil the kettle. Meanwhile, marinate the tuna in ½ tbsp of the oil, the soy sauce, some black pepper and 1 tbsp of the lemon juice.
2. Put the remaining oil and lemon juice, the capers, chives and some salt and pepper into a large bowl, mix together and set aside.
3. Pour boiling water from the kettle into a pan, add the potatoes and some salt and boil for 15 minutes, adding the beans for the final 4 minutes.
4. When the vegetables are nearly ready, heat a griddle pan until very hot then cook the tuna steaks for 1 minute on each side (if they are very thick or if you prefer them well-done, they will need a little longer). Rest on a plate while you drain the vegetables.
5. Toss the vegetables with the dressing and serve with the tuna.

Prawn, watercress & spinach salad

Illustrated on the following pages

Serves 4

400g cooked king prawns with tails
85g watercress, stalks removed
150g sugar snaps, halved lengthways
225g baby spinach leaves
3 spring onions
1 large firm, ripe mango
1 large lime
1½ tbsp fresh coriander, leaves only

For the dressing

3 tbsps Thai fish sauce
juice of 1 lime
1 tbsp caster sugar
1 medium red chilli, deseeded and finely chopped
1 thumbnail-sized piece ginger, peeled and finely grated
1 large clove garlic, peeled and finely chopped
3 tbsps groundnut or vegetable oil

1. Put the prawns in a large bowl, leaving all or a few of the tails on. Add the watercress and sugar snaps to the bowl together with the spinach leaves.
2. Trim the spring onions, halve them lengthways, then slice them on the diagonal into small pieces and add them to the bowl.
3. Slice the 'cheeks' off either side of the mango stone, peel them, and slice the flesh into long thin slivers. Remove the flesh from the stone and slice that, too. Add the mango slices to the bowl.
4. Pare the skin and pith from the lime, then chop the flesh into small pieces and put in the bowl, followed by the coriander leaves.
5. In a jug, whisk together all the dressing ingredients. To serve, toss the salad ingredients together with the dressing and serve immediately.

This dish is lightly spiced, but if you want the dressing to have a real kick, leave the seeds in the chilli.

Strawberry & langoustine salad

Serves 4

50g pine nuts

3 generous slices fresh pineapple

12 cooked langoustines

2 Little Gem lettuces, leaves separated

450g strawberries, washed, hulled and quartered

For the dressing

2 tbsp red-wine vinegar

3 tbsp extra-virgin olive oil

1 tsp clear honey

1 tsp Dijon mustard

½ tsp salt

1. Toss the pine nuts in a large dry pan over a medium heat for 4–5 minutes, until golden brown. Set aside to cool completely.

2. Meanwhile, make the dressing by whisking all the ingredients together. Set aside.

3. Slice the pineapple into segments of a similar size to the strawberries.

4. Peel the langoustines, reserving a couple of whole ones to garnish.

5. Toss the lettuce leaves and fruit with the dressing and arrange in a bowl. Put the peeled langoustines on top and arrange the langoustines still in the shell on the side. Sprinkle with the pine nuts to serve.

Langoustines are increasingly known as Dublin Bay prawns. You could use prawns instead of langoustines.

Sweet chilli prawn & egg noodle salad

Serves 4

2 blocks dried fine egg noodles (about 130g)
4 celery sticks, finely sliced on the diagonal
150g radishes, thinly sliced
300g beansprouts
400g cooked and peeled king prawns
4 tbsp sweet chilli sauce, plus more to serve
salt and freshly ground black pepper

1. Put the egg noodles in a large bowl. Pour over a kettle of boiling water and cover with clingfilm. Set aside for 5 minutes, stirring halfway, until just softened. Drain, run under cold water to cool, then drain again and tip into a large bowl.
2. Add the celery, radishes, beansprouts and king prawns to the noodles.
3. Drizzle with sweet chilli sauce, season and toss everything together until combined. Divide between plates and serve with extra sweet chilli sauce to drizzle over.

Crab, avocado & pink grapefruit salad

Serves 4

55ml olive oil
juice of 1 lemon
100g rocket leaves
2 medium avocados, sliced
1 pink grapefruit, peeled and segmented
3 whole crabs, white meat only
salt and freshly ground black pepper
10 chives, snipped, to serve

1. In a small bowl, mix together the oil, lemon juice and a little seasoning.
2. In another bowl combine the rocket, avocado, grapefruit and crabmeat. To serve, divide between four plates, drizzle with the dressing and garnish with the snipped chives.

Good quality pink grapefruit will have a smooth, firm and shiny skin. Choose a fruit that is medium to large and heavy for its size.

Seafood salad with lime & chilli salsa

Illustrated on the following pages

Serves 6

large handful of fresh parsley

1kg live mussels, cleaned and debearded (discard open ones that do not close when tapped, and any with cracked shells)

500g raw tiger prawns, peeled and deveined with tail-shells on

300g fresh prepared squid, cleaned and cut into rings or strips

2 tbsp avocado oil

juice of 1 lime

1 small shallot, finely chopped

100g rocket leaves

For the lime and chilli salsa

finely grated zest of 1 lime

1 garlic clove

1 small red chilli, halved and deseeded

large handful fresh mint

1. Put 100ml of water in a large pan. Tear the stalks from the parsley (reserve the leaves for making the salsa) and add to the pan with a couple of black peppercorns. Bring to the boil, then add the mussels, cover and cook for 5 minutes, shaking the pan until all the shells have opened. Remove the mussels with a slotted spoon, discarding any that haven't opened.

2. Add the prawns and squid to the pan, cook for 2 minutes or so until both are cooked. Remove with a slotted spoon.

3. Boil the liquid in the pan until reduced by half, then spoon about 3 tbsps of it (avoid the pepper and stalks) into a bowl and leave to cool. Discard the remaining liquid.

4. Whisk the avocado oil and lime juice into the reserved cooking liquid. Season and stir in the shallot.

5. Shell the mussels and toss with the prawns and squid. Cover and chill.

6. To make the salsa, put the lime zest, garlic and chilli in a blender and whiz until chopped. Add the mint and reserved parsley leaves and whiz to make a fine mixture.

7. Toss together the seafood with the shallot dressing, then gently fold in the rocket. Divide between serving bowls. Spoon over some lime and chilli salsa.

Smoked fish salad

Serves 4

125g hot smoked trout, flaked
225g smoked mackerel, flaked
125g hot smoked salmon, flaked
½ red onion, peeled and sliced
8 trimmed radishes, sliced
1 ripe avocado, peeled and cut into chunks
20g fresh chives, snipped
6 tbsps mustard dressing or French dressing (see the recipes on pages 111 or 172)
salt and freshly ground black pepper

To serve

crusty bread and butter to serve
50g baby spinach leaves

1. In a large serving bowl combine all the ingredients together – be careful not to break up the fish pieces too much, you want them to be fairly chunky.
2. Pour over the dressing, season and serve with some crusty bread and butter and a little baby spinach leaves on the side.

Warm salad of smoked salmon & pancetta

Serves 4
250g crispy mixed salad leaves
1 ripe avocado, diced
150g smoked salmon
130g cubed pancetta
6 tbsp French dressing (see the recipe on page 172)

1. Divide the salad leaves between serving plates, add the avocado and mix together carefully.
2. Tear the smoked salmon into rough strips and scatter over the plates.
3. Dry-fry the pancetta in a frying pan for 3–4 minutes until crisp, then add the honey and mustard dressing and let it bubble briefly. Spoon over each plate and serve immediately.

The combination of the smoked salmon with warm pancetta make this a satisfying and substantial main meal.

Peppered mackerel with vegetable crisps

Serves 2

3 tbsp extra-virgin olive oil
1 tbsp lemon juice
150g green beans
130g mixed salad leaves
2–3 smoked peppered mackerel fillets
150g cherry tomatoes, halved
40g crushed vegetable crisps
salt and freshly ground black pepper

1. Make a simple dressing by whisking the extra-virgin olive oil with the lemon juice, season and set aside.
2. Cook the beans in boiling salted water for 2–3 minutes, until just tender, then refresh under cold water, drain and cut in half.
3. Tip the salad leaves into a large bowl and add the beans.
4. Peel off the skin from 2–3 smoked peppered mackerel fillets and tear the flesh into bite-sized pieces. Add to the salad with the cherry tomatoes.
5. Add the dressing and toss well. Divide between large plates and scatter with a handful of crushed vegetable crisps to serve.

Herring with potato, beetroot & dill salad

Serves 2
250g new potatoes
75ml crème fraîche
1 dsp wholegrain mustard
1½ tbsp fresh dill, snipped into small sprigs
150g marinated herring with fresh lemon
200g cocktail beetroot
salt and freshly ground black pepper

1. Halve or quarter any larger potatoes and cook them all in a pan of boiling salted water until tender.
2. Meanwhile, mix together the crème fraîche, mustard and dill (reserve a few sprigs to serve), and season with salt and pepper. Arrange the herring on two plates.
3. Drain the potatoes and then tip them into a bowl and, while still hot, gently mix them with the beetroot and drizzle with the dressing. Serve with the herring and sprinkle over the reserved dill.

This will also work well using other oily fish, such as smoked trout or mackerel fillets.

Haddock, crispy bacon & spinach salad

Serves 4

3½ tbsp olive oil
8 slices smoked streaky bacon, cut into 1cm pieces
500g white haddock fillet, skin removed
4 eggs, at room temperature
1 tbsp white-wine vinegar
½ tsp wholegrain mustard
120g baby spinach leaves
salt and freshly ground black pepper

1. Heat a large non-stick frying pan and add 1½ tbsp of the oil. Put the bacon in the pan and cook over a high heat for 5–8 minutes, until crisp.
2. Remove with a slotted spoon onto kitchen paper and set aside.
3. Pour away a little of the oil, add the haddock to the pan and cook over a high heat for 4–5 minutes on each side, or until just cooked through.
4. Meanwhile, add the eggs to a pan of boiling water, return to the boil, then simmer for 4½ minutes. Drain the eggs, allow to cool slightly, then peel.
5. In a small bowl, mix the remaining oil, vinegar, mustard and seasoning and toss with the spinach leaves and crispy bacon. Divide between plates and put pieces of the haddock on the salad. Top with the soft-boiled egg, broken open with a knife, and serve.

salads chicken, duck & game

Chicken, red onion & green beans

Serves 4

350g fine green beans, trimmed
5–6 tbsps olive oil
2 medium red onions, peeled and each cut into 8 wedges
4 chicken breasts, skins removed and sliced into strips
juice of 1 lemon
2 tbsp small capers, rinsed
50g wild rocket leaves
80g fresh shaved Parmigiano Reggiano
salt and freshly ground black pepper

1. Preheat a griddle and bring a pan of salted water to the boil for the beans.
2. Brush the griddle with oil and cook the onions for a few minutes on each side. Meanwhile, cook the beans for 3–4 minutes or until tender. Drain and put in a large bowl. Mix with the cooked onions.
3. Season and griddle the chicken strips in 2 batches for 3–4 minutes on each side or until cooked through, adding more oil if needed.
4. Meanwhile, in another bowl, whisk together the lemon juice and 4 tbsps of olive oil, then add this mixture to the beans and onions. Add the chicken to the bowl as it is cooked. Toss everything together with the capers and rocket and arrange on four plates, scattering with Parmigiano Reggiano.

Chicken & mango with chilli lime dressing

Serves 4

8 tbsp olive oil
juice of 1 lime
1 Thai red chilli, deseeded and chopped
3 tbsp roughly chopped fresh coriander
2 small ripe mangoes
4 chicken breasts
150g mixed salad leaves
salt and freshly ground black pepper

1. Make the dressing by mixing together 6 tbsp olive oil, lime juice, chilli and coriander. Season and set aside.
2. Meanwhile, cook the chicken. Heat a griddle pan to a medium heat. Brush the chicken breasts with the remaining 2 tbsp olive oil and when the griddle is hot place the chicken in the pan and cook for 6–8 minutes each side until charred and golden and the chicken cooked through.
3. Peel the mangoes and cut into slices. Slice the chicken diagonally into thick strips.
4. Divide the salad between four plates and top with the mango and chicken slices. Drizzle over the dressing to serve.

The chilli in this dressing is a perfect match for the sweet mango. If you prefer a milder taste, use larger red chillies.

Chicken, asparagus & avocado salad

Serves 2

250g asparagus, trimmed
2 chicken breasts, skins removed
generous pinch dried chilli flakes
3 tbsp chopped fresh flat-leaf parsley
200g natural yogurt
1 tbsp vegetable oil
1 avocado, peeled and chopped
120g baby spinach leaves
50g rocket leaves
2 tbsp hemp seeds
salt and freshly ground black pepper

1. Simmer the asparagus for 2–3 minutes in salted water in a frying pan, then drain and cut the spears in half. Dry the pan.
2. Place the chicken between layers of clingfilm and flatten with a rolling pin. Season with salt and chilli. Mix the parsley into the yogurt and season.
3. Heat the oil in the pan and fry the chicken for 3–4 minutes on each side over a medium-high heat until cooked through.
4. Slice the chicken, toss with the asparagus, avocado, spinach, rocket and a drizzle of the pan juices. Scatter with hemp seeds and serve with the yogurt.

Crispy chilli chicken salad

Serves 2

¼ cucumber
2 spring onions, finely shredded
2 cooked, skinless chicken breasts
2 tbsp olive oil
2 tbsp hot chilli relish
juice of 1 lime
1 tbsp chopped fresh coriander
1 Little Gem lettuce, leaves separated
2 spring onions, finely shredded
1 lime, cut into wedges, to serve
salt and freshly ground black pepper

1. Scrape out and discard the seeds from the cucumber using a teaspoon. Chop and set aside.
2. Tear the chicken into bite-sized pieces. Heat a pan until hot, then add the olive oil. Fry the chicken for 5 minutes, stirring, until it is hot and crispy at the edges.
3. Take off the heat and stir through the chilli relish and lime juice. Put into a bowl, toss with the cucumber and coriander. Season to taste.
4. Serve on Little Gem lettuce leaves topped with the shredded spring onions and lime wedges.

Moroccan chicken & potato salad

Serves 6

750g waxy new potatoes
1 tbsp fresh lemon juice
6 tbsp extra-virgin olive oil
2 tbsp chopped fresh mint
2 red chillies, deseeded and finely chopped
120g spring onions, chopped
1 tsp Spanish smoked paprika
4 large chicken breasts, skins removed and cut into wide strips
salt and freshly ground black pepper

1. Cook the potatoes in boiling salted water for 12–15 minutes, until just tender. Drain well and quarter each potato. Put into a large bowl.
2. Whisk together the lemon juice, 4 tbsp oil, the mint and chillies. Season with salt and pepper. Pour over the potatoes then leave to cool. Stir in the spring onions.
3. Mix the remaining oil with the paprika. Add the chicken and mix well.
4. Preheat the grill. Lay out the chicken on a foil-lined tray and cook under the grill for 8–10 minutes, turning once. Toss the chicken with the potato salad and serve.

This makes a wonderful al fresco lunch and is great for the barbecue. Cook the chicken for 8–10 minutes and mix with the potato salad.

Chicken & crunchy tortilla salad

Serves 2
130g mixed salad leaves
1 cooked chicken breast, shredded
1 crisp red onion, sliced
2 handfuls of spicy tortilla chips
125g baby plum tomatoes, quartered
3 tbsp roasted red pepper dressing
3 tbsp crème fraîche or soured cream

1. Divide the salad leaves between two bowls and add the shredded chicken.
2. Scatter a few slices of red onion over the top and add the tortilla chips and quartered tomatoes.
3. Make an instant salad dressing by mixing together equal quantities of roasted red pepper dressing and crème fraîche or soured cream. Drizzle over the salad and serve.

For an alternative dressing, whiz a few strips of roasted red peppers into some red-wine vinaigrette or use the Caesar salad dressing on page 182.

Thai chicken salad

Serves 4

1 tbsp olive oil
450g chicken breasts, skins removed and cut into bite-sized pieces
1 small onion, very finely chopped
2 garlic cloves, crushed
2 tbsp soy sauce, plus extra to serve
2 tsp caster sugar
1–2 Thai red chillies, deseeded and very thinly sliced
1 cucumber
2 large carrots, cut into very thin strips
150g beansprouts
3 tbsp coarsely chopped fresh mint
3 tbsp coarsely chopped fresh coriander leaves
40g roasted salted peanuts, chopped (optional)
grated zest and juice of 1 lime, plus wedges to serve

1. Heat the olive oil in a wok or large frying pan and stir-fry the chicken pieces over a high heat for 3-4 minutes. Add the chopped onion and garlic and stir-fry for a further 2 minutes. Add the soy sauce, sugar and sliced chillies and stir-fry for 3–4 minutes more, until the chicken is brown and the sauce has reduced to a sticky glaze.
2. Meanwhile cut the cucumber in half lengthways, scoop out the seeds with a teaspoon and discard, then slice on the diagonal. Toss with the chicken. Add the remaining ingredients and stir to combine.
3. Serve with lime wedges to squeeze over, and extra soy sauce for drizzling.

Vietnamese minted chicken salad

Serves 4

2 carrots, grated
large handful fresh beansprouts
large handful fresh mint, plus extra leaves to garnish
2 shallots, finely sliced
2 small red chillies, deseeded and finely sliced, plus an extra sliced chilli with seeds to garnish
3 cooked chicken breasts, finely sliced

For the dressing

2 garlic cloves, crushed
2 tbsp brown sugar
1 tbsp rice vinegar
juice of 2 limes
1 tbsp fish sauce
4 tbsp vegetable oil
freshly ground black pepper

1. Put the carrot, beansprouts, mint leaves, shallots and chillies in a large bowl and gently toss together. Set aside.
2. For the dressing, put the garlic, sugar, rice vinegar, lime juice, fish sauce, vegetable oil and some freshly ground black pepper into a small bowl and whisk together well.
3. Divide the salad between four bowls. Add the sliced chicken, toss well and drizzle with the dressing. Garnish with the extra mint, chilli and seeds.

You can also use warm chicken in this dish. Quickly stir-fry thin strips in a little olive oil until lightly brown and crispy at the edges.

Five-spice duck salad with chicory & pears

Illustrated on the following pages

Serves 4
2 duck breasts
1 large ripe pear
2 small heads chicory, large leaves torn
120g herb salad
freshly ground black pepper

For the marinade
2 tbsps soy sauce
1 tbsp clear honey
½ tsp Chinese five-spice
freshly ground black pepper

For the dressing
3 tbsps extra-virgin olive oil
1 tbsp balsamic vinegar
1 tbsp soy sauce
1 clove garlic, peeled and finely chopped
2.5cm piece fresh ginger, peeled and finely chopped
½ tsp clear honey
juice of ½ lime
freshly ground black pepper

1. Using a sharp knife, score a diamond pattern into the duck breasts, then marinate them in the soy, honey, five-spice and some black pepper for at least 10 minutes but preferably a couple of hours, covered, in the fridge.
2. Preheat the oven to 200°C (fan 180°C), gas 6. Heat a non-stick frying pan until very hot. Wipe off as much of the marinade as you can from the chicken and place the breasts, skin-side down, in the pan. Sear them until they are brown. Turn the heat down to low and let the fat render out slowly (about 10 minutes). The skin on the duck breasts will end up crispy.
3. Place the duck on a baking tray and roast for 10 minutes, skin-side up, then let the breasts rest out of the oven for 10 minutes. Slice them thinly.
4. Place the dressing ingredients, together with a generous grinding of black pepper, in a lidded jar. Shake well to combine and set aside.
5. Peel, quarter and core the pear, then cut into thin slices. Season with freshly ground pepper.
6. Arrange the chicory and herb salad on four serving plates and divide the sliced duck and pears between them. Just before serving, shake the dressing again and drizzle over the salad.

Chinese duck, orange & noodle salad

Serves 4
125g dried medium egg noodles
2 tbsp toasted sesame oil
2 oranges
300g Chinese stir-fry vegetables
½ head shredded Chinese leaf
2 large duck breasts
1 tsp Chinese five-spice
salt and freshly ground black pepper

1. Cook the noodles in boiling water for 3–4 minutes. Drain well and tip into a large bowl. Toss with the sesame oil.
2. Cut off and discard skin and pith from the oranges. Segment the oranges into the bowl of noodles. Squeeze any excess juice from the membranes into the bowl. Add the stir-fry vegetables and the shredded Chinese leaf to the bowl. Toss everything together. Season to taste and set aside.
3. Heat a frying pan over a medium heat. Rub the duck breasts with the Chinese five-spice, then season. Cook for 5 minutes, then turn and cook for a further 5 minutes for pink meat, or longer if you like your meat well done. Lift onto a plate and leave to rest for 10 minutes.
4. Slice the duck on the diagonal. Divide the noodle salad between four plates and top with slices of duck breast.

Spiced pigeon with roast butternut squash

Serves 4

8 pigeon breasts
3 tbsp thick Greek yogurt
3 tbsp olive oil
½ tsp ground ginger
½ tsp ground cumin seeds
½ tsp salt
½ tsp hot paprika, preferably smoked
1 medium butternut squash (600g)
2 red onions, sliced
juice of 1 lemon
2 tbsp pumpkin seed oil or extra-virgin olive oil, plus extra to serve
handful of wild rocket leaves
2 tbsp butter
salt and freshly ground black pepper

1. Put the pigeon breasts, Greek yogurt, 1 tbsp olive oil, ginger, cumin, salt and paprika in a shallow ceramic dish and marinate for at least 2 hours, preferably overnight.
2. Preheat the oven to 200°C (fan 180°C), gas 6. Leaving the skin on, cut the squash into rings or half-moon slices, whichever is easiest. Toss the pieces in the remaining olive oil and add a little salt. Lay the slices, spaced well apart, on a baking sheet and cook in the oven for 25 minutes, or until slightly browned and crispy at the edges. (If you bake them this way the skin is very edible, like a jacket potato.)
3. Meanwhile, toss the sliced red onions in a bowl with the lemon juice and the pumpkin seed oil or extra-virgin olive oil. Season lightly. Gently mix the onion with the squash and rocket leaves to make a warm salad.
4. Heat the butter in a wide-based frying pan and sear the pigeon breasts for about 3 minutes on each side. Remove from the pan and set aside to rest for a good 5 minutes.
5. Cut each pigeon breast into three and serve with the butternut squash salad and extra pumpkin seed oil, if you like.

You could use duck breasts instead of pigeon. If you do, increase the total cooking time to about 10 minutes.

Pheasant, apple, fennel & orange salad

Serves 2–3
2 cold roasted pheasant breasts
1 small flavourful apple (Braeburn or Cox's)
½ bulb fennel, finely sliced
1 small orange
1 head chicory
85g watercress
50g walnut pieces

For the dressing
1 tsp grainy mustard
1 tsp runny honey
3 tbsps live natural yogurt
1½ tbsp cider vinegar
½ tsp ground coriander
55ml light olive oil
salt and freshly ground black pepper

1. To make the dressing, put the mustard, honey, vinegar and ground coriander in a bowl and whisk together. Gradually add the oil until you have a thick dressing. Now add the yogurt, whisk thoroughly and season with salt and black pepper.

2. Separate the leaves from the chicory and place them in a bowl of iced water. Score the orange skin into quarters with a sharp knife, place in a bowl and cover with boiling water. Leave for 2–3 minutes, then rinse with cold water. Remove skin and pith, and cut the orange into small segments.

3. Cut the pheasant breasts into strips. Drain the chicory and pat dry with kitchen paper. Quarter, core and slice the apple.

4. Arrange the watercress in a shallow serving bowl, scatter over half the chicory and fennel. Arrange pieces of pheasant, apple, orange, fennel and chicory alternately round the bowl. Finally, drizzle over half the dressing and scatter with walnut pieces. Serve the remainder of the dressing in a small jug for those who would like extra.

This recipe uses only the pheasant breasts. Save the legs and carcass to make a dark, rich stock that would be a great base for an onion or chestnut soup.

salads veggie

Little Gem, mushroom, apple & celery salad

Serves 4

3 celery sticks, thickly sliced diagonally, leaves reserved to serve
6 spring onions, finely shredded
4 Little Gem lettuces, cut in half lengthways
125g closed cup chestnut mushrooms, wiped clean and cut into 3 slices
2 tbsp extra-virgin olive oil
1 Cox's apple
salt and freshly ground black pepper

For the mustard dressing

1 tsp Dijon mustard
pinch of sugar
1 tbsp cider vinegar
4 tbsp extra-virgin olive oil

1. Put the celery leaves and shredded spring onions into a bowl of cold water. Put the Little Gem lettuce in another large bowl of cold water. This will help keep everything crisp.

2. To make the dressing, mix the mustard, sugar and vinegar in a small bowl, then season and whisk in the oil, a little at a time, until thick.

3. Sprinkle the sliced mushrooms with a little salt and black pepper. Heat the oil in a frying pan and, when hot, seal the mushrooms on both sides for about 1 minute. Tip into a large salad bowl and mix in 1 tbsp of the dressing. Leave to marinate for 15 minutes.

4. Cut the apple into quarters and core, then cut each quarter into 8 slices. Add the apple slices and celery to the mushrooms. Dry the Little Gem lettuce and mix into the salad.

5. Drain the celery leaves and spring onions, pat dry and fold half into the salad with the remaining dressing. Scatter the other half over the salad and serve immediately.

Couscous, broad beans, peas, mint & Feta

Serves 4–6
225g couscous
4–5 tbsp extra-virgin olive oil
225g fresh or frozen broad beans
225g fresh or frozen peas
4 plum tomatoes, deseeded and finely chopped
4 tbsp chopped fresh mint
150g Feta, crumbled
salt and freshly ground black pepper

1. Put the couscous into a large bowl and gradually stir in 300ml warm water until it is all absorbed. Leave to stand for 10–15 minutes until the grains are tender and plump.
2. Stir in 1 tbsp olive oil and rub the grains between your fingers to break up any lumps.
3. Cook the broad beans and peas in boiling salted water for 5–6 minutes, until just tender. Refresh under cold running water. Drain well and remove the tough outer skin from the broad beans. Add the beans and peas to the couscous and stir together.
4. Stir in the tomatoes and chopped mint. Season the remaining olive oil well and pour over the couscous, using a fork to distribute it. Stir in the Feta. Spoon into separate bowls or on to a platter and serve.

Potato, watercress & apple salad

Serves 6

1kg new potatoes
5 tbsp pine nuts
3 tbsp pumpkin seeds
325g low-fat natural yogurt
zest of 1 lemon
2½ tbsp lemon juice
2 tbsp manuka or other clear honey
2 cored and diced eating apples
2 handfuls watercress leaves (stalks discarded)
1 stick celery, sliced
salt and freshly ground black pepper

1. Halve the new potatoes (or cut into three if large) and simmer in salted water for 10–15 minutes until tender. Drain and cool.

2. Heat a frying pan and when it is hot toast the pine nuts with the pumpkin seeds, until golden.

3. In a large bowl, mix together the yogurt, lemon zest, 1½ tbsp lemon juice and the honey. Stir in the potatoes, pine nuts and pumpkin seeds. Toss the apple in the remaining 1 tbsp lemon juice, add to the potato and mix well.

4. Add the watercress leaves and celery. Season well and serve.

Roast pepper & garlic salad with hazelnuts

Serves 4
2 large red peppers
2 large yellow peppers
1 large garlic bulb, cloves whole and unpeeled
3 tbsp olive oil
1 tsp salt
2 handfuls oregano or marjoram, leaves picked
1 tbsp sherry or balsamic vinegar
100g whole hazelnuts

1. Preheat the oven to 200°C (fan 180°C), gas 6. Cut the peppers lengthways into rough quarters, discarding any seeds and pith, but leaving the stalks on. Lay them on baking trays skin-side up.
2. Scatter the peppers with garlic, olive oil, salt, oregano and sherry or balsamic vinegar, and cover with foil. Roast for 20 minutes.
3. Remove the foil and return to the oven for another 15 minutes, or until wilted – their skins should be brown and wrinkly. (Leave the oven on to roast the nuts.) Set aside for at least 15 minutes.
4. Meanwhile, spread the hazelnuts in a single layer on a baking sheet and cook in the oven for 5 minutes until golden. Remove and cool slightly, then roughly crush in a pestle and mortar.
5. Transfer the peppers, garlic and the juices to a serving bowl, then scatter the lightly crushed nuts over the top. Squeeze the garlic out of its skin with your fingers as you eat the salad.

This dish is great on its own or served with a softish, mildish cheese or some oily fish, such as mackerel.

Greek salad

Serves 6

1 cucumber, halved lengthways, deseeded and diced
1 large onion, thinly sliced
6 plum tomatoes, cut into chunks
24 pitted Greek black olives, halved
225g Feta, diced
1 head cos lettuce, roughly torn

For the dressing

2 tbsp fresh lemon juice
6 tbsp extra-virgin olive oil
1 garlic clove
2 tbsp fresh oregano or thyme
salt and freshly ground black pepper

1. Put the diced cucumber, onion, tomatoes, olives and Feta into a large serving bowl. Toss in the torn lettuce leaves.
2. Whisk the dressing ingredients together with plenty of seasoning and pour over the Greek salad to serve.

This is such a simple, fresh salad that can be made in next to no time. Source some really good-quality ripe tomatoes as they will have a sweet, rich flavour.

Roasted baby vegetable salad with croûtons

Serves 2–3
1 red onion, cut into wedges
75g baby carrots
75g baby sweetcorn
6 tbsp olive oil
½ garlic and rosemary flatbread
1 tbsp red-wine vinegar
120g herb leaf salad
75g mangetout
salt and freshly ground black pepper

1. Preheat the oven to 220°C (fan 200°C), gas 7. Put the red onion wedges into a roasting tin. Add the carrots and sweetcorn (halve them if they are quite large). Drizzle with 2 tbsp olive oil, season and toss together. Roast for 20 minutes, turning halfway, until just tender.
2. Tear the garlic and rosemary flatbread into chunky croûtons, add these to the vegetables then toss together. Roast for a further 8–10 minutes, until the vegetables are lightly charred and the croûtons crisp.
3. Meanwhile, whisk together the remaining 4 tbsp olive oil, the red-wine vinegar and some seasoning.
4. Put the herb leaf salad into a large serving bowl, along with the reserved mangetout. Add the roasted vegetables and croûtons, drizzle with the dressing and gently toss together. Divide between bowls to serve.

Grilled spring onions, radish & cottage cheese

Serves 4
250g cottage cheese
120g spring onions
extra-virgin olive oil, for drizzling
1 small cucumber
1 small cos lettuce or 2 Little Gem, washed and roughly shredded
200g small radishes
12 whole mint leaves
salt

For the dressing
juice of 1 lemon, plus a little zest
3 tbsp extra-virgin olive oil
1 tsp Dijon mustard
salt and freshly ground black pepper

1. Drain the cottage cheese in a sieve to get rid of any excess whey.
2. Meanwhile, trim the spring onions of any wilted greens. Heat a frying pan or griddle and dry-fry them for about 30 seconds to 1 minute each side. Drizzle with olive oil and season with salt. Set aside on a plate.
3. Make the dressing by whisking all the ingredients together in a small bowl. Season well and set aside.
4. Peel and halve the cucumber lengthways. Run a teaspoon along the seed cavity to remove the seeds and discard. Finely slice the cucumber, then toss together with the lettuce, radishes, spring onions, mint and dressing. Scatter the cottage cheese curds over the salad to serve.

Look out for the flamboyant French breakfast radish: bright pink with a white strip at the base. If the leaves look fresh, toss them into the salad as well – they taste like rocket. This is great stuffed into pitta.

Warm veg salad

Serves 4

1kg butternut squash
1 red onion, cut into 8 wedges
2 peppers, deseeded and cut into large pieces
1 tbsp fresh thyme leaves, plus extra sprigs to garnish
1 large garlic clove, crushed
2 tbsp olive oil
50g wild rocket leaves
1 tbsp balsamic glaze
100g Feta, crumbled

1. Preheat the oven to 200°C (fan 180°C), gas 6. Peel and deseed the squash and cut into eight thick wedges or large chunks. Put into a roasting tin with the onion and peppers. Add the thyme leaves, garlic and olive oil and toss well to coat. Pop the roasting tin in the oven for 45 minutes, or until the vegetables are tender and lightly charred.
2. Transfer the vegetables (including any juices) to a large serving bowl. Toss through the wild rocket and balsamic glaze.
3. To serve, divide the warm salad between four plates and scatter the crumbled Feta over the top. Garnish with the extra thyme.

Any leftover squash makes a great addition to mashed potatoes. Boil it with the potatoes, drain, and mash with some seasoning and grated Parmesan.

Five bean salad with shallot & quails' eggs

Illustrated on the following pages

Serves 4

125g mung beans, soaked overnight
200g frozen broad beans
2 shallots, sliced
juice of ½ lemon
150g fine green beans
150g Romano beans or stringless green beans, sliced diagonally
410g can red kidney beans, rinsed
12 quails' eggs, hard-boiled and halved (optional)
4 wheat tortillas, cut into wedges, to serve
a little sea salt

For the dressing

1 banana shallot or 2 round shallots, finely chopped
juice of ½ lemon
3 tbsp extra-virgin olive oil
1 large mild green chill, deseeded and finely chopped

1. Drain the mung beans and place in a large pan of fresh cold water. Bring to the boil and simmer for 10 minutes, then add a little salt and cook for a further 5 minutes, or until tender. Drain and set aside until needed.
2. Boil the broad beans in salted water for 4–5 minutes, until tender, then drain and plunge into cold water. Drain again, then remove and discard the tough white skins to reveal the bright green beans. Set aside.
3. Put the sliced shallots into a bowl with the lemon juice and set aside.
4. Meanwhile, make the dressing. Put the chopped shallot and lemon juice into a large salad bowl and leave for 10 minutes. Whisk the oil into the shallots, a little at a time, then stir in the chilli and a little sea salt to taste.
5. Add the mung and broad beans to the dressing and mix together.
6. Put the green and Romano beans into a pan of boiling salted water and simmer for 4 minutes. Drain and refresh under cold water. Add to the salad with the kidney beans and mix together.
7. Drain, rinse and dry the sliced shallots, then top the salad with the shallots and quails' eggs, if using. Brown the tortilla wedges on a griddle pan and serve with the salad.

Runner bean, tomato & pesto salad

Serves 6
600g runner beans
50g pine nuts
180g cherry tomatoes, quartered
75g sun-blush tomatoes in oil, drained, cut into strips
25g rocket leaves
3 x 100g small goats' cheese rounds
12 thin slices French bread, cut on the diagonal from a baguette
olive oil, for drizzling

For the pesto dressing
½ tsp Dijon mustard
1 tsp white-wine vinegar
2 tbsp extra-virgin olive oil
2 tbsp fresh pesto
salt and freshly ground black pepper

1. Bring a pan of lightly salted water to the boil. Top and tail the runner beans, then remove the strings from each side. Cut on the diagonal into 1cm slices. Drop into the boiling water and cook for about 5 minutes or until just tender. Drain, refresh in cold water, and drain well again.
2. Preheat the grill to high. Pop the pine nuts onto a baking tray and toast under the grill for 2 minutes, until golden. Set aside to cool.
3. Mix the runner beans, cherry and sun-blush tomatoes, pine nuts and rocket together in a bowl.
4. Make the dressing. Whisk the mustard and vinegar together, then slowly whisk in the oil. Stir in the pesto and season.
5. Discard the top and bottom of each cheese round and cut each into four slices. Grill the bread slices for 2 minutes. Turn over and grill for 1 minute, then drizzle with a little oil. Top each with a cheese slice, and grill until just beginning to melt.
6. Toss the dressing into the salad and spoon onto plates. Lay two warm cheese croûtes alongside each salad to serve.

This has a lovely combination of textures with crisp, fresh salad and the warm creamy goats' cheese croûtes.

salads
sides

Salad with toasted mixed seeds

Serves 6

1 head radicchio
2 Little Gem lettuces or 1 cos lettuce
2 heads red or white chicory
150g radishes, trimmed and finely sliced
3 tbsp ready-toasted mixed seeds, such as sunflower, pumpkin and sesame
salt and freshly ground black pepper

For the dressing

4 tbsp olive oil
juice of 1 lime
1 tsp light muscovado sugar

1. Carefully break up all the salad leaves and the chicory. Wash well and dry. Place in a large serving bowl and add the sliced radishes.
2. Mix all the ingredients for the dressing together and pour over the leaves. Sprinkle with the toasted seeds and add a pinch of salt and plenty of freshly ground black pepper. Toss well and serve.

This is a crunchy salad that will add interest to simple chicken and fish dishes, and the lime dressing is wonderfully refreshing.

Warm barley salad with butternut squash

Illustrated on the following pages

Serves 4

1 large butternut squash, peeled, deseeded and cut into 3cm-cubes
2 tbsp olive oil
250g pearl barley
200g fine green beans, trimmed and halved
1 medium red onion, peeled and finely diced
3 stalks celery heart, finely sliced
3 tbsp roughly chopped fresh mint leaves
4 tbsp roughly chopped fresh parsley
100g goats' cheese
salt and freshly ground black pepper

For the dressing

8 tbsp extra-virgin olive oil
1 clove garlic, peeled and finely chopped
½ tbsp dried crushed chillies
6 tbsp red-wine vinegar
1 tbsp runny honey
salt and freshly ground black pepper

1. Preheat the oven to 180°C (fan 160°C), gas 4. Spread the pieces of squash over a baking tray, drizzle with the olive oil and season. Bake in the oven for 20 minutes, remove and set aside.

2. Meanwhile, rinse the barley, then cook in plenty of boiling, salted water for about 20–25 minutes, or until just tender. In a separate pan, cook the beans in boiling water for 3–4 minutes.

3. To make the dressing, warm the oil in a pan, add the garlic and chilli and lightly brown over a low heat. Allow to cool slightly, then add the red-wine vinegar, honey and some seasoning. Whisk until combined.

4. Drain the barley and beans and place in a large bowl. Add the onion, celery and cooled squash. Pour the dressing over the salad and gently mix together. Add the herbs, mix again, then crumble the goats' cheese on top.

Courgette som tam

Serves 4

2 medium courgettes, trimmed
1 medium carrot, trimmed
100g French green beans, topped and tailed
2 garlic cloves, chopped
1–2 small red chillies, deseeded and sliced lengthways
salt and freshly ground black pepper

For the dressing

2 tbsp Thai fish sauce
juice of 2 limes
1 tsp sugar or honey
salt and freshly ground black pepper

To serve

1 large handful fresh coriander leaves, as a garnish
100g roasted peanuts, roughly crushed

1. Using a potato peeler, peel the courgettes along their length, then keep going, making strips of the flesh until you reach the seed pod in the centre. Discard the seed pod. Peel the carrot in the same way. Put the vegetables in a large bowl.
2. Blanch the green beans in plenty of boiling salted water for no longer than a couple of minutes, until they are just tender. Drain and rinse in cold water. Add to the bowl of vegetables, along with the chopped garlic and sliced chilli.
3. Make the dressing. Mix the fish sauce, lime juice and sugar, then season to taste. Pour the dressing over the vegetables, toss together and allow the salad to sit for a good 30 minutes before serving – this will deepen the flavour and have the effect of slightly 'cooking' the carrot and courgette.
4. Divide the salad between plates. Garnish with coriander leaves and serve with the crushed peanuts separately to sprinkle over.

This would be lovely as part of a Thai-style spread, but it also goes very well with simple grilled fish or chicken dishes.

Hot potato, orange & red cabbage salad

Serves 6

400g new potatoes, scrubbed
3 blood oranges or 2 medium oranges
¼ tsp of salt
½ tsp white-wine vinegar
4 tbsp mild olive oil
1 small or ½ medium red cabbage
1 medium red onion or 1 large pink shallot, sliced into thin wedges
2 white or pink chicory
1 tbsp flat-leaf parsley, leaves removed

1. Put the potatoes into a large saucepan of cold salted water and bring to the boil. Simmer for about 12–15 minutes, or until tender.

2. Meanwhile, finely grate ¼ tsp of zest from 1 orange and set aside. Cut the peel and pith from all the oranges and segment them over a bowl to catch all the juice. Squeeze in the juice from the remaining orange membranes and set aside.

3. Put the grated orange zest, white-wine vinegar and 2 tbsp of the reserved orange juice into a large salad bowl. Whisk in the oil a little at a time, then add the orange segments.

4. Shred the cabbage into another bowl, add the red onion or shallot wedges and toss well with the remaining orange juice.

5. Drain the cooked potatoes and cut into bite-sized pieces. Toss with the dressing and oranges in the salad bowl. Drain the cabbage and shallot wedges and add to the salad bowl.

6. Cut the chicory into bite-sized pieces and add to the salad bowl. Drain and dry the parsley leaves and add to the salad. Toss well and serve while the potatoes are still hot.

New potatoes with chorizo & broad beans

Illustrated on the previous pages

Serves 4

500g Jersey Royal new potatoes
1kg broad beans to yield about 200g podded beans
2 tbsp olive oil
1 medium onion, peeled and sliced
225g chorizo de pueblo, rind removed and sliced into 1cm pieces
2 plum tomatoes, deseeded and chopped
4 tbsp chopped flat-leaf parsley leaves
2 tbsp sherry vinegar
2 handfuls rocket leaves
salt and freshly ground black pepper

1. Bring a large pan of salted water to the boil and cook the new potatoes for 10 minutes. Add the broad beans and cook for a further 3–5 minutes.
2. Meanwhile, heat the olive oil in a frying pan and soften the sliced onion for 3–4 minutes before adding the chorizo. Cook for a further 3 minutes, tossing to cook on both sides.
3. Drain the potatoes and beans, cool slightly, then thickly slice the potatoes lengthways and add to the onion mixture along with the beans, tomatoes, parsley and vinegar. Season and toss together. Add the rocket and toss once more before serving.

Serve this with some grilled or barbecued chicken or fish to make a hearty meal.

Braised peas with leeks, lettuce & mint

Serves 6
3 Little Gem lettuces or 5 Little Gem lettuce hearts
75g butter
2 small (about 150g) leeks, trimmed, washed and thinly sliced
750g frozen or freshly shelled peas
1 tbsp chopped fresh mint leaves
salt and freshly ground black pepper

1. Trim the lettuces and cut each lettuce lengthways into six wedges.
2. Melt half the butter in a deep sauté pan over a medium-low heat. Add the leeks and sauté gently for two minutes or until softened. Add the lettuces and cook for 1–2 minutes or until they begin to wilt. Add the peas and 100ml water. Season. Simmer for 3–4 minutes, stirring, until the peas are softened and about half the liquid has evaporated.
3. Dot over the remaining butter, sprinkle with the chopped mint and shake the pan briefly.

Warm pea & lentil salad

Serves 4
200g Puy lentils
2 garlic cloves
1 shallot or small onion, finely sliced
juice of 1 lemon or 2 limes
4 tbsp extra-virgin olive oil
200g peas

1. There is no need to soak Puy lentils. Just wash them and cook in plenty of unsalted water with the garlic for about 20 minutes, until they are tender but retaining some bite. You can discard the garlic at this point if you wish. Drain the lentils and place in a large serving bowl.
2. Add the shallot, lemon or lime juice and oil to the lentils and toss together. Season to taste and set aside.
3. Blanch the peas for no more than a minute or so in plenty of boiling water. Drain, add to the lentils and serve.

Try wilting some fresh herbs, such as basil, parsley, chives or mint into the salad. Toss them through the lentils before serving. You can use mangetout (snow peas), broad beans or sugar snaps instead of the peas.

Orange & watercress salad

Serves 4–6

4 oranges, preferably navel or Valencia
6 spring onions
175g watercress
2 heads chicory, broken into leaves
6 tbsp extra-virgin olive oil
salt and freshly ground black pepper

1. Using a small sharp knife, cut the top and bottom off an orange. Stand the orange on a chopping board and cut away the skin and pith, from top to bottom, in sections. Hold the orange over a bowl and cut out each segment between the membrane, letting the segment and juice fall into the bowl. Squeeze out the juice from the empty membrane. Repeat for all the oranges.
2. Strain off and reserve the juice. Put the segments into a serving bowl. Trim the spring onions and finely shred into lengths. Add to the orange segments with the watercress and chicory.
3. Take 2 tbsp of the orange juice and whisk in the oil and plenty of seasoning in a small bowl. Drizzle over the salad and toss everything together and serve.

Watercress's peppery kick complements the citrus burst of fresh orange in this salad.

A rather old-fashioned rice salad

Serves 4

300g long-grain rice
100g podded broad beans
2 spring onions, sliced
200g can tuna steak in olive oil, drained
200g freshly grated Gruyère cheese
4 ripe tomatoes, deseeded and chopped
8 pickled cornichons
8 baby artichoke hearts in oil
100g radishes, trimmed, washed and sliced
4 tbsp extra-virgin olive oil
juice of 1 lemon
4 tbsp chopped fresh flat-leaf parsley, to garnish
salt and freshly ground black pepper

1. Wash the rice and put in a small saucepan with 450ml cold water. Cook for 15 minutes then spread the rice out over a baking tray and allow it to cool thoroughly.

2. In a large pan of salted, boiling water quickly blanch the broad beans for about 2 minutes, then shuck them from their skins by squeezing them between your thumb and forefinger.

3. Mix the broad beans, spring onions and rice in a large bowl. Fold in the tuna, cheese, tomatoes, cornichons, artichokes and radishes.

4. Whisk the olive oil with the lemon juice and fold into the salad. Season to taste and garnish with parsley to serve.

Country-style potato salad

Serves 6

550g waxy new potatoes, such as Pink Fir Apple or Charlotte
juice of ½ lemon
4 tbsp extra-virgin olive oil
2 tbsp chopped fresh oregano
1 small red onion, finely chopped
12 pitted green olives
4 plum tomatoes, deseeded and roughly chopped
2 tbsp capers
4 eggs, hard-boiled
salt and freshly ground black pepper

1. Cook the potatoes in boiling salted water for 12–15 minutes, until just tender. Drain well and cut in half. Put into a large bowl.
2. In a small bowl, whisk together 1 tbsp of lemon juice, the olive oil, oregano and plenty of seasoning. Pour over the warm potatoes and set aside.
3. When the potato salad has cooled, add the onion, olives, tomatoes and capers and toss well. Peel and roughly chop the boiled eggs and scatter over the salad. Toss the salad once more just before serving.

The addition of chopped eggs makes this a lovely alternative to a traditional potato salad.

Italian bean salad

Serves 4–6

7 tbsp extra-virgin olive oil
1 small onion, finely chopped
2 plump garlic cloves, crushed
1 stick celery, finely chopped
2 red chillies, deseeded and chopped
2 tsp chopped fresh oregano
410g can cannellini beans, drained and rinsed
410g can borlotti beans, drained and rinsed
6 plump tomatoes, deseeded and chopped
3 tbsp chopped fresh parsley
2 tbsp lemon juice
salt and freshly ground black pepper

1. Heat 3 tbsp of the olive oil in a large saucepan and cook the onion, garlic, celery and red chilli gently over a low heat for 6–8 minutes, until softened.
2. Stir in the oregano and all the beans and heat gently for 5–6 minutes, stirring occasionally. Remove from the heat and allow to cool.
3. Stir in the tomatoes and parsley. Whisk the remaining olive oil with the lemon juice and season well. Just before serving, pour over the bean mixture and toss well.

Serve this with smoky barbecued steaks, cold poached salmon or with a large mixed green salad.

Roasted baby beetroot

Serves 4
1 tsp caraway seeds (optional)
800g baby beetroot with tops
4 tbsp extra-virgin olive oil
1 tbsp balsamic or sherry vinegar
1 tbsp Dijon mustard
1 tsp sea salt

1. If you're using the caraway seeds, dry-toast in a hot pan for 30 seconds. Crush and set aside.
2. If the beetroot comes with the tops (greens), remove, wash, then blanch them for a minute in boiling water. Drain and set aside.
3. Preheat the oven to 220°C (fan 200°C), gas 7. Put the beetroot in a baking tray and toss with half the oil and a little salt. Roast for 20 minutes, until cooked through. When cooled slightly, put on clean rubber gloves and rub the beetroot skins off.
4. Whisk the remaining oil with the vinegar, mustard, caraway seeds and sea salt, then toss with the beetroot tops and roots.

If you store this in a covered container in the fridge, it keeps well for up to 2 days.

Fresh Italian parsley salad

Serves 6

50g couscous
2 sun-dried tomatoes, finely chopped
2 tbsp olive oil
grated zest and juice of 1 lemon
25g black olives, pitted and finely chopped
50g fresh flat-leaf parsley leaves
salt and freshly ground black pepper

1. Put the couscous and sun-dried tomatoes in a large heat-proof bowl and pour over 50ml boiling water. Leave to cool.
2. Stir in the olive oil, lemon zest and juice, olives and some seasoning. Toss through the parsley just before serving.

You can make the couscous and tomato dressing earlier in the day but don't mix in the fresh parsley. Put it into a bowl with the parsley leaves on top, then cover and chill. Bring back to room temperature, then simply toss the parsley through to serve.

Christmas coleslaw

Serves 6–8

200g mayonnaise (see the recipe on page 186)
150g natural yogurt
1 tsp ground cumin
500g mixed sweet and crunchy salad, or mixed shredded white cabbage and carrot
50g toasted pecan nuts, roughly chopped
salt and freshly ground black pepper

1. In a serving bowl mix together the mayonnaise, yogurt and cumin. Season to taste.
2. Add the mixed salad and toss well to coat in the dressing.
3. Just before serving, top with the pecan nuts.

A lovely rich slaw with a slight kick – ideal to accompany cold meats.

salads
fruit

Cherry & fig compote for ice cream

Serves 2

150ml port
1 small cinnamon stick
½ vanilla pod
1 rounded tbsp soft brown sugar
250g fresh cherries
2 fresh figs
good quality vanilla ice cream, to serve

1. Place the port in a pan with the cinnamon, vanilla and sugar and simmer over a low heat for 2–3 minutes, until reduced by about half.
2. Meanwhile, remove the stones from the cherries using a cherry or olive stoner and cut the figs into quarters.
3. Add the cherries to the pan and cook for 2 minutes, then add the figs and cook for a further minute. Remove from the heat and allow to cool slightly before serving with scoops of ice cream.

Citrus salad

Serves 2

2 limes

2 oranges

2 pink grapefruit

2 tbsp chopped fresh mint

a little honey, to drizzle

1. Remove the peel and pith from the limes, oranges and pink grapefruit. Slice into bite-sized pieces, reserving any juices that come from the fruit.

2. Put all the fruit in a serving dish and mix with the chopped mint and reserved juice. Drizzle with a little honey, to serve.

This light, refreshing salad is the perfect ending to a rich meal.

Autumn fruit salad

Illustrated on the following pages

Serves 6
500g ripe plums or greengages, washed and stalks removed
2–3 ripe peaches or nectarines
2 ripe dessert pears
150g fresh blackberries

For the syrup
110g golden granulated sugar
1 stick cinnamon
1 large lemon
2–3 thin slices fresh ginger

1. Start by making the syrup. Place the sugar and 150ml of water in a pan. Add the cinnamon stick, two or three pieces of the pared lemon rind and the sliced ginger. Stir over a low heat until the sugar has dissolved, then bring to a simmer. Remove from the heat and leave to infuse until cold.
2. Squeeze the lemon and add the juice to the syrup, then strain it into a large serving bowl.
3. Now prepare the fruit. Cut the plums or greengages in half, following their natural line, and remove the stones. Slice into fairly chunky pieces and add to the spiced syrup.
4. Scald the peaches, remove the skins, then halve them. Remove the stones and slice. There's no need to skin the nectarines, just halve them, remove the stones and slice. Add these to the syrup, too.
5. Peel and halve the pears. Scoop out the cores using a teaspoon. Slice the pears into quarters or eighths so you have long slivers, then add them to the syrup as well. Turn them over so that they are fully coated in the lemon juice to keep them white. Finally, add the blackberries.
6. Let everything marinate for 2–3 hours before serving – the syrup will draw out the natural fruit juices to achieve a perfect balance of flavours.

This fruit salad is very versatile; it can be served for dessert, with natural yogurt, or spooned over muesli for breakfast.

Strawberries, liqueur & mascarpone cream

Serves 4

500g small strawberries, hulled and halved
2 tbsp Cointreau or orange liqueur
finely grated zest of ½ small orange
1 tbsp icing sugar, plus 1–2 tsp for the cream
5cm vanilla pod
125g mascarpone
2 tbsp single cream

1. Put the strawberries, Cointreau liqueur, orange zest and icing sugar in a bowl and mix together gently. Cover and chill in the fridge for about an hour, until the strawberry juices have run a little. Bring it back up to room temperature.
2. Just before serving, slit open the vanilla pod and scrape out the seeds. Mix with the mascarpone, cream and some extra icing sugar to taste.
3. Serve the strawberries in dessert glasses and top with a little of the mascarpone cream.

Spiced cherries in vodka

Serves 6

450g cherries, stalks left on
400ml cranberry juice
200ml vodka
200ml apple juice
50ml cherry brandy
1 tbsp juniper berries, crushed
pinch of ground allspice

1. Prick the cherries in several places with a sterilised needle so that they will absorb the vodka mixture better.
2. Mix all the remaining ingredients together in a large jug or bowl.
3. Add the pricked cherries, cover and set aside in a cool place for anything between 1–12 hours before serving up in shot glasses.

You can serve this after 1 hour of macerating but, obviously, the longer you leave it, the more potent it will become. You could use orange liqueur in place of the cherry brandy.

Pineapple with mint & lime sugar

Serves 4
1 large ripe, sweet pineapple
50g caster sugar
finely grated zest of 1 lime
large handful fresh mint leaves

1. Carefully slice the top and bottom off the pineapple. Stand it upright on a chopping board and slice away all the skin and the little brown 'eyes'. Quarter lengthways so you have four long wedges. Slice away the woody cores from each wedge.
2. Cut the pineapple across each wedge into thin slices and arrange them in small tumblers. Cover with clingfilm and chill in the fridge until needed.
3. To serve, put the sugar, lime zest and mint leaves into the bowl of a small food processor and blitz for about 30 seconds, until the mint is finely chopped and you have a bright green mixture. Sprinkle over the pineapple in each glass and serve.

Ripe pineapples smell sweet and the leaves should pull out quite easily from the centre. Don't be tempted to make the sugar before you need it because the mint will start to go black and lose its fresh taste.

salads dressings & mayonnaise

French dressing

Serves 4

1 tbsp white-wine vinegar
1 tsp mild mustard (such as wholegrain or Dijon)
a small pinch of sugar
3 tbsp extra-virgin olive oil
salt and freshly ground black pepper

1. Put the white-wine vinegar, mustard, sugar and some seasoning into a large bowl. Whisk until well emulsified.
2. Add the extra-virgin olive oil in a slow, steady stream, whisking all the time, until cloudy and slightly thickened.

A good all-round dressing that is used throughout this book. It works well with all manner of ingredients, from chicken and steaks to smoked fish and mixed leaf salads.

Basil vinaigrette

Serves 4
6 tbsp extra-virgin olive oil
2 tbsp red-wine vinegar
15g torn basil leaves
1 small garlic clove
1 shallot, finely chopped
a pinch of sugar
salt and freshly ground black pepper

Put all the ingredients with some seasoning into the bowl of a small food processor and whiz until smooth.

A perfect addition to a simple salad of grilled fish, chicken or meat as well as tomato or new potato salads.

Poppy seed vinaigrette

Serves 4

1 tbsp poppy seeds
¼ tsp Dijon mustard
1 tbsp balsamic vinegar
3 tbsps olive oil
½ small shallot, finely chopped

1. Dry-fry the poppy seeds in a non-stick pan over a high heat for 1 minute, until lightly toasted.
2. In a small bowl, whisk the mustard with the balsamic vinegar then gradually whisk in the olive oil.
3. Add the seeds and the chopped shallot and stir well to mix together.

Use this dressing to liven up a bowl of green leaves. It is great on all leafy salads for adding a bit of crunch.

Lemon vinaigrette

Serves 4
3 tbsp extra-virgin olive oil
1 tbsp freshly squeezed lemon juice
salt and freshly ground black pepper

In a small bowl whisk the extra-virgin olive oil with the lemon juice, adding a little seasoning to taste.

Brilliant for vegetable salads, such as broad beans and Feta cheese, or beetroot.

Walnut oil dressing

Serves 4
3 tbsp walnut oil
4 tbsp extra-virgin olive oil
2 tbsp white wine vinegar
1 tsp golden caster sugar

Combine all of the ingredients in a small, lidded jar and shake together.

Walnut oil has a strong, distinct flavour and requires a hearty salad to stand up to it. Beetroot, goats' cheese and meat salads are excellent choices for this dressing.

Mediterranean dressing

Serves 4

100g marinated sundried peppers in olive oil, plus 2 tbsp of the oil from the jar
3 tbsp lemon juice
3 tbsp olive oil
1 tsp dijon mustard
10 basil leaves
6 pitted Kalamata or other black olives
1 heaped tbsp capers, drained
6–8 tbsp boiling water to loosen
salt and freshly ground black pepper

1. Put the peppers along with their oil, the lemon juice, olive oil and the dijon mustard into the bowl of a small food processor or blender and whizz for 20–30 seconds or until smooth. Season to taste. Turn into a mixing bowl.
2. Chop the capers and olives and shred the basil leaves and add to the bowl. Stir together adding the hot water gradually until the mixture has loosened to the right consistency.

Use as a dressing for roasted vegetables, couscous or new potato salads.

Classic Caesar dressing

Serves 4

1 large garlic clove
1 anchovy fillet
1 egg yolk
¼ tsp Dijon mustard
1 tbsp lemon juice
100ml mild olive oil
2 tbsp grated Parmesan
½ tbsp double cream
freshly ground black pepper

1. Crush the garlic clove under the blade of a large knife and rub it around the inside of a bowl, then discard.
2. Mash the anchovy fillet on a board with the blade of a knife and add to the bowl. Add the egg yolk, mustard and lemon juice. Whisk until smooth.
3. Slowly whisk in the olive oil, until creamy. Stir in the grated Parmesan, double cream and some pepper.

Blue cheese dressing

Serves 4
50g blue cheese (Gorgonzola is good)
2 tbsp milk
1 tbsp white-wine vinegar
6 tbsp olive oil
salt and freshly ground black pepper

Put the cheese in the bowl of a food processor along with the milk, white-wine vinegar, olive oil and a little seasoning; blend until smooth. Add a few drops of warm water if it seems a little thick.

Serve over a crunchy salad of watercress, avocado and peppery radish.

Mayonnaise

Serves 4–6
2 medium egg yolks
1 tsp Dijon mustard
300ml light olive oil
good squeeze fresh lemon juice
salt and freshly ground black pepper

1. Sit a large bowl on a cloth to stop it moving. Put the egg yolks into the bowl along with the Dijon mustard and a little seasoning and whisk well until smooth.
2. Gradually add the olive oil in a slow, steady stream, whisking all the time. You should have a smooth, quite thick mayonnaise that stands in peaks.
3. Add lemon juice to taste and briefly whisk. If it's too thick, whisk in a few drops of warm water to give a good consistency.

Fresh mayonnaise will keep, covered, in the fridge for 3–4 days.

Aïoli

Serves 6–8

6 garlic cloves, crushed
3 egg yolks
3 tbsp fresh white breadcrumbs
4 tbsp white-wine vinegar
300ml good olive oil
salt and freshly ground black pepper

1. Put the garlic cloves, egg yolks, breadcrumbs, white-wine vinegar and a little seasoning into a bowl and whisk well (or whiz in a food processor).
2. Gradually whisk in the olive oil in a slow, steady trickle (or pour through the funnel of the food processor with the motor still running).
3. Whisk in 1 tbsp warm water and check the seasoning.

Serve as a dip with fresh crudités – as well as the usual carrot sticks and celery, try strips of fennel, asparagus and radishes. Combine with cooked potatoes to create a garlicky potato salad, or use as a sauce for fish and shellfish.

Index

A
Aïoli 188
All-day-breakfast salad 16
apples: Apple & pork salad with cider dressing 50
  Potato, watercress & apple salad 114
aubergine: Lamb & aubergine with pomegranate 54
Autumn fruit salad 161
avocados: Chicken, asparagus and avocado salad 89
  Crab, avocado & crispy bacon salad 24
  Crab, avocado & pink grapefruit salad 68

B
bacon: All-day-breakfast salad 16
  BLT salad 45
  Haddock, crispy bacon & spinach salad 80
  Warm mozzarella, bacon & nectarine 43
Basil vinaigrette 174
beans: Five bean salad with shallot & quails' eggs 123
  Runner bean, tomato & pesto salad 126
  see also borlotti bean, broad beans and cannellini beans
beef: Griddled beef salad with mushrooms 35
  Griddled steak with potatoes & peppers 38
  Hot Thai beef salad 36
  Tagliata (seared steak & rocket salad) 32
beetroot: Herring with potato, beetroot & dill salad 78
  Roasted baby beetroot 152
BLT salad 45
Blue cheese dressing 185
borlotti beans: Italian bean salad 150
broad beans: Couscous, broad beans, peas, mint & Feta 112
  New potatoes with chorizo & broad beans 140
butternut squash: Spiced pigeon with roast butternut squash 104
  Warm barley salad with butternut squash 131
  Warm veg salad 122

C
cabbage: Hot potato, orange & red cabbage salad 136
Caesar dressing, Classic 182
Caesar salad, Classic 20
cannellini beans: Italian bean salad 150
  Seared tuna with bean & olive salad 59
cherries: Cherry & fig compote for ice cream 158
  Spiced cherries in vodka 167
chicken: Chicken & crunchy tortilla salad 95
  Chicken & mango with chilli lime dressing 86
  Chicken, asparagus & avocado salad 89
  Chicken, red onion & green beans 84
  Crispy chilli chicken salad 90
  Moroccan chicken & potato salad 92
  Thai chicken salad 97
  Vietnamese minted chicken salad 98
  Vietnamese salad 13
  Warm chicken & herb salad 12
chorizo: New potatoes with chorizo & broad beans 140
  Warm salad of pear, scallop & chorizo 29
Christmas coleslaw 154
Citrus salad 160
Classic Caesar dressing 182
Classic Caesar salad 20
coleslaw: Christmas coleslaw 154
cottage cheese: Grilled spring onions, radish & cottage cheese 120
Country-style potato salad 148
Courgette som tam 134
Couscous, broad beans, peas, mint & Feta 112
crab: Crab, avocado & crispy bacon salad 24
  Crab, avocado & pink grapefruit salad 68
  Zesty herb & chilli crab salad with crostini 19

D
duck: Chinese duck, orange & noodle salad 102
  Five-spice duck salad with chicory & pears 99

E
eggs: All-day-breakfast salad 16

F
Feta cheese: Greek salad 116
figs: Cherry & fig compote for ice cream 158
  Parma ham, fig & mozzarella salad 10
fish: Haddock, crispy bacon & spinach salad 80
  Herring with potato, beetroot & dill salad 78
  Peppered mackerel with vegetable crisps 77
  A rather old-fashioned rice salad 147
  Seared tuna with bean & olive salad 59
  Smoked fish salad 72
  Tuna salad with beans, capers & new potatoes 60
  Warm salad of smoked salmon & pancetta 74
Five bean salad with shallot & quails' eggs 123
French dressing 172

G
Gorgonzola: Blue cheese dressing 185
grapefruit: Citrus salad 160
  Crab, avocado & pink grapefruit salad 68
Greek salad 116

Griddled beef salad with mushrooms 35
Griddled steak with potatoes & peppers 38

H
Haddock, crispy bacon & spinach salad 80
Herring with potato, beetroot & dill salad 78
Hot potato, orange & red cabbage salad 136
Hot Thai beef salad 36

I
Italian bean salad 150
Italian parsley salad 153

L
lamb: Lamb & aubergine with pomegranate 54
Warm Sunday roast salad 52
langoustines: Strawberry & langoustine salad 64
Lemon vinaigrette 178
lentils: Warm pea & lentil salad 142
Little Gem, mushroom, apple & celery salad 111

M
mackerel, smoked: Peppered mackerel with vegetable crisps 77
Smoked fish salad 72
mangoes: Chicken & mango with chilli lime dressing 86
Mayonnaise 186
Mediterranean dressing 181
Moroccan chicken & potato salad 92
mozzarella: Parma ham, fig & mozzarella salad 10
Warm mozzarella, bacon & nectarine 43
mussels: Seafood salad with lime & chilli salsa 69

O
oranges: Citrus salad 160
Hot potato, orange & red cabbage salad 136
Orange & watercress salad 144

P
pancetta: Warm salad of smoked salmon & pancetta 74
Paprika-spiced pork 48
Parma ham: Parma ham, fig & mozzarella salad 10
Warm potato salad with Parma ham 44
parsley: Fresh Italian parsley salad 153
peaches: Autumn fruit salad 161
Tomato, peach & cumin salad 22
pears: Autumn fruit salad 161
Warm salad of pear, scallop & chorizo 29
peas: Braised peas with leeks, lettuces & mint 141
Warm pea & lentil salad 142
peppers: Roast pepper & garlic salad with hazelnuts 115
Pheasant, apple, fennel & orange salad 106
pigeon: Spiced pigeon with roast butternut squash 104
Pineapple with mint & lime sugar 168
plums: Autumn fruit salad 161
Poppy seed vinaigrette 177
pork: Apple & pork salad with cider dressing 50
Paprika-spiced pork 48
Sticky spare ribs & crunchy slaw 25
potatoes: Country-style potato salad 148
Hot potato, orange & red cabbage salad 136
Moroccan chicken & potato salad 92
New potatoes with chorizo & broad beans 140
Potato, watercress & apple salad 114
Warm new potato & smoked sausage salad 39
Warm potato salad with Parma ham 44
prawns: Prawn, watercress & spinach salad 61
Seafood salad with lime & chilli salsa 69
Sweet chilli prawn & egg noodle salad 67

R
radicchio: Salad with toasted mixed seeds 130
radishes: Grilled spring onions, radish & cottage cheese 120
Rice salad, A rather old-fashioned 147

S
Salad with toasted mixed seeds 130
salmon, smoked: Smoked fish salad 72
Warm salad of smoked salmon & pancetta 74
Warm new potato & smoked sausage salad 39
scallops: Warm salad of pear, scallop & chorizo 29
Seafood salad with lime & chilli salsa 69
spinach: Prawn, watercress & spinach salad 61
spring onions: Grilled spring onions, radish & cottage cheese 120
squid: Seafood salad with lime & chilli salsa 69
Squid, lemon & caper salad 26
Sticky spare ribs & crunchy slaw 25
strawberries: Strawberries, liqueur & mascarpone cream 164
Strawberry & langoustine salad 64
Sweet chilli prawn & egg noodle salad 67

T
Tagliata (seared steak & rocket salad) 32
Thai beef salad, Hot 36
Thai chicken salad 97
tomatoes: Tomato, fresh mint & lemon salad 18
Tomato, peach & cumin salad 22

trout: Smoked fish salad 72
tuna: A rather old-fashioned rice salad 147
Seared tuna with bean & olive salad 59
Tuna salad with beans, capers & new potatoes 60

V
vegetables: Roasted baby vegetable salad with croûtons 118
Warm veg salad 122
Vietnamese minted chicken salad 98
Vietnamese salad 13
vinaigrettes: Basil 174
Lemon 178
Poppy seed 177

W
Walnut oil dressing 180
Warm barley salad with butternut squash 131
Warm chicken & herb salad 12
Warm mozzarella, bacon & nectarine 43
Warm pea & lentil salad 142
Warm potato salad with Parma ham 44
Warm salad of pear, scallop & chorizo 29
Warm salad of smoked salmon & pancetta 74
Warm Sunday roast salad 52
Warm veg salad 122
watercress: Orange & watercress salad 144
Potato, watercress & apple salad 114
Prawn, watercress & spinach salad 61

Z
Zesty herb & chilli crab salad with crostini 19

Acknowledgements

Most of the recipes in this book were first published in **delicious.** magazine or **Sainsbury's Magazine**. We are thankful to all the staff (past and present) involved in both magazines and to those at the Seven Publishing Group for providing the material and their assistance.

Recipes by:
Felicity Barnum-Bobb 20, 167; Fiona Beckett 106; Kate Belcher 24, 67, 86, 102, 118, 126, 172, 174, 177, 178, 182, 185, 186; Angela Boggiano 19, 25, 130 Lorna Brash 48, 97; Tamsin Burnett-Hall 74, 154; Matthew Drennan 10, 13, 36, 50, 52, 59, 77, 92, 95, 98, 112, 116, 144, 148, 150, 188; Silvana Franco 69, 153; Ghillie James 16, 38, 60, 68, 80, 140, 180; Jennifer Joyce 39, 54, 99, 131; Debbie Major 44, 141, 164; Kim Morphew 90; Tom Norrington-Davies 22, 26, 29, 32, 64, 104, 115, 120, 134, 142, 147, 152; Sarah Randell 12, 35, 45, 61, 78, 84, 89, 114, 160; Annie Rigg 18, 72, 158; Natalie Seldon 43; Linda Tubby 111, 123, 136.

Photography credits:
Steve Baxter 14–15, 70–1, 88, 93, 113, 117, 145, 149, 151; Peter Cassidy 17, 34, 40–1, 55, 100–1, 132–3, 138–9; Lisa Cohen 62–3; Gus Filgate 162–3; Jonathan Gregson 146; Janine Hosegood 53; Richard Jung 46–7, 79, 85, 127, 165; Gareth Morgans 51, 66, 76, 91, 103, 119; Lis Parsons 42, 49, 96, 166; Michael Paul 110, 124–5, 137, 169; Claire Richards 21; Deidre Rooney 11, 37, 58; Clive Streeter 81, 87; Lucinda Symons 189; Lucinda Symons and Anthony Blake pic. Library 173, 175, 176, 179, 183, 184, 187; Peter Thiedeke 94; Simon Walton 73, 75, 155, 159; Cameron Watt 107; Rob White 23, 27, 28, 33, 65, 105, 121, 135, 143.